D1830888

SELECT VIEWS IN MYSORE, THE COUNTRY OF TIPPOO SULTAN

SELECT VIEWS IN MYSORE, THE COUNTRY OF TIPPOO SULTAN

FROM

DRAWINGS TAKEN ON THE SPOT

BY

MR. HOME;

WITH

HISTORICAL DESCRIPTIONS

GYAN

Published by

Gyan Publishing House
5, Ansari Road
Daryaganj, New Delhi-110002
Phone: 011-47034999, 9811692060
E-mail: books@gyanbooks.com

Distribution Network
gyanbooks.com
India, USA, Canada, UK, Australia, France

© Publisher

All rights reserved. No part of this work may be reproduced, stored, adapted, or transmitted in any form or by any means, electronic, mechanical, photocopying, micro-filming, recording or otherwise, or translated in any language, without the prior written permission of the copyright owner and the publisher.

ISBN : 978-81-212-3993-6 (PB)
First Published, 1794

2nd Impression 2020

Printed at: Gyan Press, Delhi.

The book is sold subject to the condition that it shall not, by way of trade or otherwise, be lent, resold, hired out, or otherwise circulated without the prior publisher's written consent.

Select Views in Mysore, the Country of Tippoo Sultan
Author: Mr. Home

SELECT VIEWS

IN

MYSORE,

THE COUNTRY OF TIPPOO SULTAN;

FROM

DRAWINGS TAKEN ON THE SPOT

BY MR. HOME;

WITH

HISTORICAL DESCRIPTIONS.

LONDON:

PUBLISHED BY MR. BOWYER,

HISTORIC GALLERY, PALL MALL.

THE LETTER-PRESS BY T. BENSLEY,

FROM FIGGINS'S TYPES.

1794.

TO THE RIGHT HONOURABLE

CHARLES MARQUIS CORNWALLIS,

KNIGHT OF THE MOST NOBLE ORDER OF THE GARTER,

LIEUTENANT GENERAL OF HIS MAJESTY'S FORCES,

GOVERNOR GENERAL AND COMMANDER IN CHIEF OF ALL THE BRITISH POSSESSIONS IN INDIA, &c.

THESE VIEWS IN THE MYSORE COUNTRY,

WITH HISTORICAL DESCRIPTIONS,

ARE, WITH HIS LORDSHIP'S PERMISSION,

MOST RESPECTFULLY INSCRIBED,

BY HIS LORDSHIP'S

MOST OBEDIENT AND OBLIGED

HUMBLE SERVANT,

HISTORIC GALLERY, PALL MALL,
1794.

R. BOWYER.

PREFACE.

Whatever tends to increase the sphere of man's knowledge is unquestionably important, and in this respect history and geography have a conspicuous claim to our attention. Since the year 1497, when Vasco de Gama discovered a passage to India round the Cape of Good Hope, the southern coasts of Asia have been repeatedly visited by an uninterrupted succession of navigators from the different maritime states of Europe. For a long time, however, these were merely plunderers or merchants, prompted solely by the love of gain, or the spirit of enterprize; which once gratified, they had no farther object. At length, not contented with the precarious benefits derived from occasional voyages, though often highly lucrative, they began to extend their views, and form permanent establishments, for the enjoyment of a constant and settled trade.

Amongst these more politic adventurers the english soon distinguished themselves; till a simple band of merchants, from the possession of a few petty factories, established in India an empire so powerful as to give laws to it's native princes. Still our geographical knowledge of this country, which in ages past probably diffused science throughout the world, as of late it has administered to it's luxury, was nearly confined to it's shores: and this to such a degree, that the names of paltry towns to which Alexander had extended his arms were far more familiar to us, than those of provinces of which the revenues flowed into our own coffers. Now indeed science hails the dawn of a more propitious era. Asia holds in it's bosom natives of Britain, who feel more gratification from an increase of knowledge, than an increase of wealth; and from whom therefore we may hope the amplest additions to the general store.

For our parts, we pretend not to add much to the stock of information, though we tread almost unbeaten ground. It is our province to stimulate curiosity, not to gratify it. This we leave to abler pens: and we do it with the more satisfaction, as the speedily promised work of major Dirom will undoubtedly afford a rich banquet to every one who thirsts after science; and to this we must beg leave to refer, for a fuller account of the places, of which we have given views, than was consistent with our plan.

Yet we trust we have not been uselessly employed, in presenting to the public this sketch, as a tribute of respect to that able commander, and those gallant officers, by whom the british dominion in the east has been preserved from the utter destruction with which it was threatened. Aspiring to the foundation of a new empire in India, and the extension of the mohammedan faith over those parts of Asia, where to the crescent no homage had ever been paid, the politic and ambitious Hyder Ali, and his no less politic and ambitious successor, were well aware, that the power of Britain could by no means accord with their designs. Totally to expel from Indostan, therefore, a potent band of strangers, whom they could never hope to reduce under their sovereignty, or subject to the moslemim creed, was an indispensable preliminary to an accomplishment of their grand purpose.

Unfortunately for themselves, they had to do with an enemy too politic, and too powerful. Their ambitious dreams have vanished; and the present sultan of Mysore has found himself compelled to relinquish half his dominions, as a security that he would no more attempt to disturb the tranquillity of his neighbours.

Of some of the leading events of this glorious war, into which we were by necessity impelled, it is our intention to give a concise yet faithful sketch: and whilst we do this, we presume the annexed views of places, for the accuracy of which we can vouch, and in engraving which no expence has been spared, will be highly gratifying to those to whose eyes such scenes are not familiar, and not less so to those who will recognize in them the places where they gallantly fought and conquered.

VIEW of the INSIDE GATE at BANGALORE with the GUARD ROOM.

Published as the Act directs by R. Bowyer, Historic Gallery, Pall Mall, London, [illegible] at Madras, Feb. [illegible]

Home del.^t Morris sculp.^t

EAST VIEW of BANGALORE with the CYPRESS GARDEN.

Published as the Act directs by R. Bowyer Historic Gallery Pall Mall London, & J. Sharp, at Madrass Feby 1. 1794.

Home del.t Fittler sculp.

VIEW of the PETTAH GATEWAY, where COLONEL MOORHOUSE fell.

Published as the Act directs by R. Bowyer, Historic Gallery, Pall Mall, London, & W. Sharp, Madras, Feb.y 1794.

Home del. Lowry sculp.

INSIDE VIEW of the PALACE at BANGALORE.

Published as the Act directs, by R. Bowyer, Historic Gallery, Pall Mall, London; & W. Sharp, at Madrass, Feb.y 1, 179[illegible]

Home del.   Hawksworth sculp.

VIEW OF THE DELHI GATEWAY AFTER IT WAS REPAIRED.

Published as the Act directs by R. Bowyer Historic Gallery Pall Mall London & W. Sharp Madras Feb.y 1st 1791

NORTH VIEW of BANGALORE from the PETTAH, shewing the Curtain & Bastions that were breached.

SOUTH VIEW of BANGALORE, one Mile & a half distant on the Road to Seringapatam.

Home, delt. 1 2 3 4 5 6 7 Fittler sculp.

VIEW of the BURIAL GROUND at BANGALORE.

Published as the Act directs by R. Bowyer, Historic Gallery, Pall Mall, London, & W. Sharpe, Madrass, Feb. 1. 1794.

MONUMENTS

ERECTED TO THE MEMORY OF THOSE BRAVE OFFICERS WHO FELL AT THE TAKING OF BANGALORE, &c.

As it was not possible in so small a space to engrave the inscriptions on the Monuments in the annexed platė, the Reader will please to observe the figures underneath the View refer to the following inscriptions.

N° 1. Interred the remains of lieutenant Conan, of the madrass artillery, who died in storming the pettah of Bangalore, march 7th, 1791.

2. Sacred to the memory of lieutenant-colonel Gratton, quarter-master-general of his majesty's forces in India, who died 31st december, 1791.

3. To the memory of captain James Smith, of the bengal artillery, who died october 24th, 1791, aged 33.

4. Captain James Williamson, of the first battalion of bengal volunteers, and commandant of Bangalore, died february 20th, 1790. His brother, and the other officers of the corps, with equal and joint zeal, erect this monument to his memory.

5. Sacred to the memory of captain John Slipper, who fell in the service of his country, 18th march, 1791.

6. Sacred to the memory of captain Nathaniel Dawes, commandant of the fourth battalion of N. I. who died march 25th, 1791.

7. To the memory of captain Jeremiah Delany, of his majesty's 36th regiment, who gallantly fell in storming the pettah of Bangalore, march 7th, 1791.

بنکالور

شهر بنکالور بسیار کشاده است قلعه سورت دایره طولاني دارد و خوب محکم است اول شهر و قلعه معمور هندوان بودند لیکن زیادتي کرفته اند بحکم نولب حیدر علي و تیپو سلطان تیپو اینجا دولت خانه عالي شان بناکرده اند الحال صد سال کذشته که در تصرف راجه میسور امده است دراین اثنا قوم مرهته دوبار شهرا کرفته اند اول بهدایت هندو راو بار دیکر بهدایت کوپال راو صاحب کلان انکریزان نواب ارل کارنوالس بهادر روز پنجم ماه مارج سال ١٧٩١ انکریزي محاصره بنکالور فرموده بودند روز٧ هجوم اورده شهرا کر فتند و شب روز٢١ هجوم اورده قلعه‌را کرفتند

BANGALORE.

Bangalore, the capital of a province of the same name, in the kingdom of Mysore, is situated in latitude 12° 57′ 30″, and in longitude 77° 22′ 17″ east from Greenwich. From Madras it is distant two hundred and twenty-one miles, and from Seringapatam seventy-seven. Of the surrounding country the elevation is considerable; for the mercury in the barometer is always below twenty-seven inches. It's climate may justly be deemed temperate, as the thermometer commonly stands at 70°, has been sometimes observed below 60°, and seldom rises higher than 85°. The soil is not deficient in fertility, being capable of producing most of the vegetables of Europe in abundance and perfection.

The pettah, or town, is of considerable extent; being two thousand yards long, by seven hundred and fifty broad, within the fortifications, which consist of a rampart, a thick hedge, and a deep dry ditch. These do not completely surround the place, it being left open at the part opposite the fort, to the north of which it is situated.

The fort is of an oval figure; extending somewhat more than nine hundred yards in it's longest diameter. It is fortified with a broad double rampart, about thirty semicircular bastions, or turrets, and five cavaliers. There are two entrances to it; one at each end. That on the north, called the Delhi gate, consists of five strong, large gates, finished with considerable elegance: that on the south, called the Mysore gate, consists of four only, low, and far inferiour to the others in beauty. Both these gates are covered with outworks. The ramparts of the fort are extremely well built: the ditch is deep, and wide, but dry in most parts of it: the faussebraye and covert way are both very broad.*

Originally built by the hindus, as some figures sculptured in the walls, and an ancient pagoda in the middle of the place, sufficiently evince, it has been considerably altered and improved in the modern style by Hyder Ali and Tippoo Sultan; who have added many outworks, and by whom the Delhi gate has been entirely rebuilt. They likewise established here a mint, a foundry for brass cannon, a machine for boring them, another for musket barrels, which will bore a hundred and thirty at once, an arsenal for military stores, and magazines for grain and gunpowder.

Though these are in point of utility the most important, the most splendid fabric within the walls is the palace built by Tippoo for his own residence. This is grand and spacious, displaying to the four winds of heaven as many ample fronts, each composing a lofty hall, the wooden roof of which is supported by colonnades of the same material. The pillars are connected by scolloped arches; and the whole is superbly painted and gilt. The walls in front of the entrances to the east and west halls have balconies, richly carved, and raised by small pillars, united by arches. In the middle of each balcony is a square projection, which we suppose to have been intended for the seat of state, whenever the Sultan held a durbar. The north and south fronts are extremely airy, no wall dividing them, so that the eye com-

* For a plan of the fort and pettah, see plate 30, at the end of the book.

pletely pervades the building. In front of each face of the palace is a fountain: and on the north, south, and west, are jenanas, not yet finished, low, but highly ornamented with painting and gilding. Opposite the north and south fronts are small flower gardens, on the right and left, in which the pink of Europe vies with the variegated flowers of the east.

With regard to the ancient history of Bangalore much information cannot yet be expected. About the middle of the seventeenth century it belonged to a poligar rajah, named Kempy Gowr, from whom it was taken in 1655 by Remdoula Khan, a general of Audil Shaw, king of Bejapour. By him it was left in charge to Shahajee, the father of Sewajee, from whom it devolved to Yekojee, one of his sons. Cassim Khan, a general of Aurung-zebe, investing it in 1689, Yekojee surrendered the place, and retired to Tanjore; after which it was sold by Cassim Khan to the Mysore rajah. About the year 1730, a mahratta army under Hindoo Row, attacked it, and took the pettah, but failed of success against the fort. In 1746 the mahrattas again besieged it, under Gopaul Row. On this occasion the pettah was once more taken, batteries were erected, and a breach was made in the fort; but a sum of money induced the assailants to desist from pursuing their enterprise farther.

Bangalore was deemed a place of great importance at the beginning of the late war: but, as our commander in chief was desirous if possible to bring the enemy to a decisive action in the open field, it's attack was not determined upon, till it plainly appeared, that Tippoo was too prudent to stake his fortune on the event of a general engagement. Thus it was late in 1790 before the siege of this place was resolved on, and early in 1791 earl Cornwallis took the command of the army, avowedly with the intention of attacking it. He began his march from Vellout on the 5th of february; on the 20th the whole of his forces had ascended the ghauts, by the Muglee pass; and on the 5th of march the army was encamped before Bangalore.

Tippoo, having been deceived into a firm belief, that his lordship meant to take the road of the Barramaul valley, had fortified the Changamah pass in that quarter, and made dispositions to prevent our army from ascending the ghauts there. To call our general's attention homewards too, already had he begun to ravage the Carnatic, and had even taken Permacoil. Astonished when he found himself so egregiously duped, and learnt, that the british forces, having without interruption surmounted the formidable barrier opposed by nature to their progress, were rapidly penetrating into his dominions; he found himself compelled to abandon his purpose, and repair with speed to the protection of his own country. Marching with incredible diligence, he arrived near Bangalore on the same day with our army, and made a show of offering battle: but lord Cornwallis, not deceived by this feint, opposed to him his left wing only, while the right, covering the battering train, baggage, and stores, pursued it's march. The enemy began a cannonade at a great distance; which, as they did not advance, was not returned. In the evening the whole army encamped within three miles of the fort; and next morning took a more convenient position on the north east of the pettah.

The same morning the fort and pettah were reconnoitered; and in the afternoon another reconnoitering party went out, escorted by colonel Floyd, with the whole cavalry, and a brigade of infantry. The colonel, observing the rear of Tippoo's army at a great distance from the main body, pursued and attacked it with the horse, and made himself master of some guns: but a body of infantry advantageously posted behind some rocks, which he had not observed, galled him severely, and obliged him to retreat. He was himself wounded, and his loss was considerable, chiefly owing to the badness of the ground.

It being on many accounts desirable for our forces to have possession of the pettah, it was resolved not to defer it's attack. Accordingly the king's 36th regiment, and the 26th battalion of bengal sepoys, under the command of lieutenant-colonel Cockerell, with a body of artillery under lieutenant-colonel Moorhouse, were ordered to storm it the following morning.

On the 7th, at dawn, they advanced to the north gate, which had been fixed on as the point of attack. The first barrier was soon penetrated, and they rushed on to the second, but were opposed there by a well directed and close fire of musketry from the walls, accompanied by showers of ground rockets, which did considerable execution. A six-pounder was run up with it's muzzle to the gate; but it's explosion had no other effect than making a small hole. A second time it was fired with no better success. At this critical juncture fell the gallant Moorhouse. As he was giving directions for an iron twelve-pounder to be brought up, he received a ball under his left shoulder, and almost instantaneously expired. Still the attack was continued with undaunted perseverance, and the gate being at length considerably shattered by reiterated explosions, it was forced open, and the whole detachment rushed in. The enemy fled from the gate, but continued firing from the houses for some time. Parties were sent in different directions to dislodge them; and before nine we were in complete possession of the place. Captain Delany, of the 36th, was killed at the beginning of the attack, and our loss altogether amounted to about a hundred men.

In the afternoon Tippoo made an attempt to dislodge us, and

three kushoons of his infantry entered the pettah, at the opening on the south, which we have already noticed. Marching in regular divisions, their attack was conducted with great spirit, whilst Tippoo advanced from the north-west side of the fort, and cannonaded our main army. The steady bravery of our troops, however, reinforced with the 76th regiment, compelled them to retreat, with the loss of their standards, and at least five hundred men.

Our batteries were soon after begun, and on the 12th three of them opened on the fort, with considerable effect on the defences, but too distant for making a breach. Two others were erected therefore, about four or five hundred yards from the works. These soon demolished the stone facing; but the solid body of the rampart, which was of red clay, crumbled but slowly.

On the 17th Tippoo again cannonaded our camp, from the heights on the north-east, but at too great distance to occasion any serious mischief.

On the 21st he once more attempted to interrupt our operations, appearing with his army on the east side of the fort, and seeming to meditate an attack on our batteries. He had likewise opened embrasures in the bank of a tank, in which he had planted some heavy cannon, that would have enfiladed our trenches. His right wing and rear, however, being exposed to the attack of one of our wings, which made a movement towards him, he drew off, leaving part of his guns behind him. Thus had he now made an attack from each of the three open quarters, and found them equally unsuccessful.

Notwithstanding the heavy and well directed fire from the fort, from which the mud walls and other cover in the pettah greatly protected our troops, the breach was now practicable; and accordingly it was resolved to storm the fort without delay. The flank companies of all the king's regiments, under the command of major Skelly, and supported by some battalions of sepoys, were ordered upon this service.

Colonel Maxwell commanded the attack, which commenced about eleven o'clock. The fort, in a moment, was completely illumined by a number of blue lights suspended from the ramparts, for the purpose of discovering the assailants; a practice very common in indian camps and garrisons. These lights exhibited to the camp a striking and interesting scene, during the mounting of the breach, and the climbing over the different parts of the gateway, which was a principal object of the attack. The grenadiers with their usual intrepidity first ascended the breach, clearing the way with their bayonets, and dispersing the enemy with great slaughter. Thence they proceeded along the rampart to the right, whilst the light infantry took the contrary direction, and the rest of the troops descended into the body of the place. They all met near the opposite gate, which the fugitives in their tumultuous retreat had now choked up, and a horrible scene of carnage ensued. The killahdar, or governor, Bahaudar Khan, a venerable old soldier, and a favourite of his master, fell, bravely fighting to the last, near the colours of his fort. Above six hundred of the garrison shared his fate; three hundred, most of them wounded, were made prisoners; and near two thousand are said to have escaped. Our loss was only about fifty officers and men, killed and wounded.

The body of the killahdar was found the next day, amidst a heap of slain, and pierced through and through with balls and bayonets. Earl Cornwallis sent a message to Tippoo, with an offer of the corpse for interment; to which the latter with equal spirit and prudence replied, that the proper place for the burial of a soldier was the spot where he fell. In consequence the body was buried in the fort, by people of the mussulman religion, and with every mark of distinction.

If we consider the circumstances attending the siege, that the enemy was in full possession of the open country, so as to preclude the possibility of our getting supplies, that during our operations in the pettah we had but a small force in the camp to withstand the attacks of their whole army, and that both our provision and ammunition were nearly exhausted, the capture of Bangalore may be deemed one of the greatest achievements of the british arms in India. Nor will it's importance be diminished, if we advert to it's consequences. Independent of the immediate advantages accruing to us from the possession of a post and magazine so important, and the consequent loss, disappointment, and disgrace to the enemy, it was attended with others, which, though more remote, were not less beneficial: for by furnishing an unequivocal proof of our superiour prowess and military skill, it operated to our advantage equally in the camps of our allies, and in the garrisons they were then besieging; the spirits of the former rising, whilst those of the latter were proportionally depressed. More strongly was it evinced by the immediate revolt of Tippoo's new subjects, the Poligars, in the vicinity of our conquest: they not only bringing in provision to the army, but even seizing on some of Tippoo's ill-garrisoned forts; as if they anticipated his approaching fall.

Since Bangalore has been in our possession, elegant monuments have been erected in the cemetry, to the memory of the officers who fell at the taking of the fortress, and in it's vicinity.

Home del. — Fittler sculp.

DISTANT VIEW of SAVENDROOG.

Published as the Act directs by R. Bowyer Historic Gallery, Pall Mall, London; & W. Pope, Madras, Feb 7, 1794

Home del. *Medland sculp.*

DISTANT VIEW of SAVENDROOG, two days March from BANGALORE.

Published as the Act directs, by R. Bowyer, Historic Gallery, Pall Mall, London; & W. Sharp, at Madrass, Feb. 1792.

Home del. Skelton sculp.

NORTH VIEW of SAVENDROOG from MAUGREE.

Published as the Act directs by R. Bowyer, Historic Gallery, Pall Mall, London, & W. Sharp, Madrass, Feb. 1. 1792

ساوندروک

ساوندروک کوهي است از سنک عظیم و بلند محفوظ به دیوار هرجا که دخل تواند بود متفرق به دو سر بر هر یک جنکلي کرداکردش کوههاي سنکین و بیشه است ازاین جهت مطلقا حصین دانسته شده دیو راوز راجه میسور ساوندروکرا بحیله برد از پولیکار نام کهپي کاور سال یک هزار هفت صد و سي

روز دهم ماه دسبر سال یک هزار هفت صد نود ویک فرقه از لشکر ارل کارنوالس تابع حکم کرنل ستوارت محاصره اینجاکرد روز بیست و یکم بحمله برداشت و در لشکر انکریزي کسي نکشته شد

SAVENDROOG.

THIS stupendous fortress, situated nineteen miles nearly west by south from Bangalore, enjoys such advantages from nature, as to need little assistance from art; though art seems to have neglected nothing to render it absolutely impregnable. It is a vast mountain of rock, supposed to rise above half a mile in perpendicular height, from a base of eight or ten miles in circumference.

Completely surrounded by walls, and defended by cross walls and barriers wherever it was deemed accessible, it has the farther advantage of being divided above by a vast chasm, separating it into two hills; each of which having it's own defences, two distinct citadels are formed, capable of being maintained independant of the lower works. Beside all this, added to the rocky hills and natural forest thickened with clumps of planted bamboos, which constitute no easily surmountable barricade, the pestiferous atmosphere threatens with inevitable destruction the hardiest troops, should they lie long before it. Hence it's significant appellation of Savendroog, or the Rock of Death. So confident indeed was Tippoo Sultan in it's strength, that he was highly pleased when he heard the british troops had run their heads against the tremendous Gurdun Shekô, a name he had himself given it, implying the Neck of Majesty; and his courtiers even congratulated him on the event, as on a victory.

About the commencement of the present century Savendroog belonged to an independant chieftain, or poligar, named Kempy Gowr, from whom it was taken by treachery in 1730, by Deo Rauze, rajah of Mysore, after a long siege.

In the lower fort or pettah were some time confined twenty british officers, and thirty soldiers, taken prisoners by Hyder Ali. Whilst they were here, Ameen Sahib was sent hither by his nephew, Tippoo Sultan, who had succeeded to the throne, and was kept for some days without food in a small enclosure on the top of the rock. He broke loose, but was soon retaken; and, being tied hand and foot, in a standing posture, to a stake driven into the ground, he was thus exposed for some time to the scorching sun, till an order arrived for the bowstring to put a period to his existence and his sufferings. This example before their eyes, with the accounts they frequently received of the murder of their fellows in other prisons, tended by no means to cheer our countrymen in their confinement: but the treaty of Mangalore taking place in the beginning of 1783, they heard the glad tidings of peace, and soon after experienced the happiness of revisiting the territories of the british empire.

Towards the end of the year 1791, lord Cornwallis, having to wait in this part of the country for convoys from the Carnatic, judged it a favourable opportunity to attempt the reduction of Savendroog; as it's remaining in possession of the enemy would have been a considerable impediment to the success of his grand enterprize. Posting therefore the main body of his army in such a situation as to support the attack, and cover an important convoy he expected; and three detachments, under lieutenant-colonel Cockerell, captain Welch, and captain Alexander Read, on the northern, middle, and southern roads; he entrusted the execution of this arduous enterprize to lieutenant-colonel Stuart, who commanded the right wing of the army, and had been employed, in the first campaign, in reducing the forts of Dindigul and Palgautcherry.

On the 11th of december the colonel pitched his camp within three miles of the north side of the rock, the quarter from which the chief engineer had proposed to carry on the attack. His force consisted of the 52d and 72d regiments, commanded by lieutenant-colonel Nesbitt, three battalions of sepoys, and a detachment of artillery under major Montagu, with a park of four eighteen-pounders, four twelves, two howitzers, and the field pieces of the corps.

To cut a gun-road from the encampment, and transport the artillery to the foot of the mountain, over rocky hills, and through a thick forest of bamboos, required incredible exertion: but to patient zeal and persevering ardour what is impracticable? By the 17th the work was accomplished, and two batteries were opened; one at a thousand, the other at seven hundred yards distance. The defences of the wall were much damaged, and the fire of the enemy was in great measure silenced by these: but the difficulty of making a breach was greater than was expected, the wall being built of immense stones, of which the lower tier was bound to the rock by clamps of iron.

On the 19th opened an advanced battery, which it had been found necessary to erect within two hundred and fifty yards of the wall; and before the lapse of the succeeding day a practicable breach was effected. The forest, through which the troops had cut their way with such labour, now became an advantage; as under cover of it, and of crevices and projections in the rock, a lodgment was made within twenty yards of the breach.

The flank companies of the 71st and 76th regiments having been sent from camp to join the detachment, and every thing being in readiness, the morning of the 21st of december was fixed for the assault. Lord Cornwallis came, accompanied by general Medows, to witness the success.

Lieutenant-colonel Nesbitt commanded the storming party, which was directed to four different attacks. Captain Gage, with the grenadiers of the 52d, and the flank companies of the 76th, to gain the eastern hill to the left: the honourable captain Monson, with the light company of the 52d, to scour the works towards the western hill, on the right: the honourable captain Lindsay, and captain Robertson, with the flank companies of the 71st regiment, to separate, and attack the works or parties they might discover in the chasm or hollow between the hills: the 52d and 72d regiments were to follow the flank companies. At the same time parties were detached round the mountain, under lieutenant-colonel Baird, and major Petrie, to draw the attention of the enemy from the main object, and to endeavour to prevent their escape.

At eleven o'clock, a signal of two guns being fired from the batteries, the troops advanced to the assault; the band of the 52d regiment playing 'Britons, strike home!' while the grenadiers and light infantry mounted the breach.

A large body of the enemy had been observed, in the morning, to come down from the western hill, for the defence of the breach: but on the appearance of the british soldiery advancing to the storm, they were seized with a panic, and fled. Our troops advanced as rapidly as the ruggedness of the rock, and the steepness of the ascent would permit; and the eastern hill, immediately above the breach, was carried by captain Gage, without meeting, or even overtaking the enemy.

The other division and main body of the enemy endeavoured to gain the western hill. Had this been effected, the siege must have recommenced; that part of the mountain being defended by several walls and barriers, whilst in most places it is of a precipitous steepness. On these accounts it was impossible to entertain any very sanguine hopes of getting possession of it immediately: captain Monson was left to his discretion, therefore, either to advance, if he found it adviseable, or to take post where the ground might favour a lodgment for attacking the works.

The pathway from the breach to the western hill being not only extremely steep, but narrow, the fugitives impeded each other; and a few well directed shots from the batteries, at that juncture, did execution, and increased their confusion. Captain Monson, with his own light company of the 52d regiment, and a serjeant and twelve grenadiers of the 71st, pressed so hard, that they entered the different barriers along with the enemy, killing a number of them, among whom was the second killahdar; and gained possession of the top of the mountain, where the head killahdar was made prisoner. So close and critical was the pursuit, that the serjeant of the 71st, when at some distance, shot the man who was shutting the first gate.

Above a hundred of the enemy were killed on the western hill, and several fell down the precipices in their endeavours to escape from the assailants. The prisoners were few. According to their report, the garrison had consisted of fifteen hundred, but many deserted during the siege.

Thus, in less than an hour, in open day, the stupendous and hitherto deemed impregnable fortress of Savendroog was taken by storm, without the loss of a single man killed, and only one private soldier wounded; and his arm was carried away by a cannon ball from one of our own batteries, rebounding from the rock, as he ascended to the assault.

VIEW of MAUGREE PAGODAS.

Published as the Act directs by R. Bowyer Historic Gallery, Pall Mall, London & W. Sharp, Madrass, Feb. 1. 1794

بتخانه ماکري

این بتخانهها در میان ساوندروک و اوتراندروک میباشند عمارات عالي و خوب سورت لیکن از مدتي ویرانه در حال شکست ریخت میشوند شهر ماکري کلان بود و در کردش دهات در سال یک هزار هفت صد و سي راجه دیو راوز این شهرا به جنک اوردند صاحب کلان ارل کارنوالس دو بار در این مکان خیمه زدند در جنک تیپو سلطان

MAUGREE PAGODAS.

These Pagodas are situated in latitude 12° 57′ 25″ south; twenty-four miles west from Bangalore; about five miles and half, north west by west half west, from Savendroog; and nearly the same distance east from Outradroog. The fort lies a mile and a quarter from them east south east.

Lofty, and of elegant structure, they are built on an eminence, commanding a fine prospect of the country around: but they have long been abandoned, and are falling into decay. Within the square which encloses them are several choultries, the walls and cielings of which are adorned with curious paintings and sculptures. In them are depicted under a variety of allegorical forms the hindu deities; particularly the god Vishnu, whose numerous actions, and several incarnations, are minutely displayed: and these monuments of their worship are still held in veneration by the remaining brahmins, and people of the hindu religion.

The town of Maugree was large and surrounded with villages: and these superb pagodas, the smaller ones in every village, the swamey houses, or hindu temples, on every eminence, even on the pinnacles of the droog, and the numerous large tanks that water the adjoining country, testify it's having been once a rajahship of great note. But war and conquest have altered it's features.

Of it's history we know nothing previous to the year 1730, when Deo Rauze, the rajah of Mysore, took it by assault, and annexed this territory to his dominions, as he did many others.

On the 28th of june, 1791, lord Cornwallis pitched his camp here, whilst he reconnoitered Savendroog. On the 24th of december he encamped here again, and waited for the detachments by which Outradroog, Ramgurry, and Shevagurry, were attacked and taken. And in this neighbourhood his lordship was joined by the forces of the soubah, or nizam, on the 25th of january, 1792.

Home del. Byrne sculp.

SOUTH VIEW of the WORKS and PETTAH of OOTRADROOG.

Published as the Act directs by R. Bowyer, Historic Gallery, Pall Mall, London, & W. Sharp, Madrass, Feb.y 1, 1794

SOUTH WEST VIEW of OOTRADROOG.

Published as the Act directs by R. Bowyer, Historic Gallery, Pall Mall, London, & W. Page, Madras, Feb.y 179[illegible]

اوتراندروک

اوتراندروک یکي از قلعجات حصین ملک میسور است
فرقه از لشکر کرنل ستوارت بزیر حکم کپتان سکات
اوتراندروک‌را بحمله برد سه روز بعد گرفتن ساوندروک
و در این کارزار سیواي و کسی دیگري زخمي
نشد

OUTRADROOG.

OUTRADROOG, one of the many strong fortresses of the Mysore country, in which a small intrepid band might long keep a large army at bay, is about eleven miles distant from Savendroog, towards the west north west, and thirty west from Bangalore.

Hither were sent at the commencement of the late hostilities twelve of the crew of the Hannibal, whom admiral Suffrein basely delivered into the hands of Hyder Ali, during that war, in which Britain had alone to contend with the forces of the east and west, aided by the arms of her neighbours in Europe. From this place they contrived to escape, one dark and rainy night, down the precipices on the north side of the rock, at the expence of a few bruises, and one broken arm. But they were unfortunately discovered the next day, by a boy keeping cattle, who conveyed information of their track to the garrison. Finding themselves pursued, they separated: seven were retaken; two arrived safe in the british territories; of the other three no tidings have ever been heard.

The recaptured fugitives could expect nothing but the severest treatment; and indeed of six of them famine soon put a period to the existence. The seventh, Mr. Cadman, a midshipman, must soon likewise have perished from inanition, had not the army of lord Cornwallis passed this way; when fear probably induced the killahdar to supply him with a sufficiency of wholesome nourishment. This soon recruited his strength, and enabled him to be removed to Seringapatam, where he was liberated about six months after by his victorious countrymen.

On the march of the army from Seringapatam to Bangalore, in june 1791, this fortress was summoned to surrender. The killahdar tauntingly answered: " I have eaten Tippoo's salt for twenty years, and will not give up my post till you have taken Seringapatam."

He was unable however to keep his word; for though lord Cornwallis judged it not adviseable to attack the fortress at this time, he sent against it, on the 23d of december following, lieutenant-colonel Stuart's detachment, flushed with the capture of Savendroog.

The killahdar, being again summoned, appeared to persist in his resolution; and to avoid any communication, fired on the flag of truce. Colonel Stuart in consequence made his disposition to attack the lower fort and pettah* next morning. Captain Scott, of the bengal establishment, with four battalion companies of the 52d and 72d regiments, and his own battalion of sepoys, was sent on this service, while another body made a feint, and opened some guns on the opposite side of the fort.

So rapidly did captain Scott carry the lower fort by escalade, that the killahdar sent to request a parley. While this took place, an appearance of treachery was observed in the upper fort, the garrison being busily employed in moving guns, and bringing them to bear on the assailants.

* For a plan of the fort and pettah, see the end of the work.

Exasperated at this sight, and impatient of the delay, the troops again rushed on to the assault. Lieutenant M[c]Innes, of the 72d regiment, led the storm, with part of the europeans, and the pioneers, commanded by lieutenants Dowse and Macpherson; supported by captain Scott, who followed in more regular order with the rest of his force.

Some of the gates were burst open, others escaladed; till, having passed five or six different walls, which defended this steep and difficult rock, the troops at length gained the summit. So infatuated were the enemy, that whenever they saw a single european above the walls they fled: and although, from the steepness and narrowness of the road in the ascent, a few men of determined courage might with ease have stopped the progress of the assailants, they attempted not to make the least resistance; except at the last gateway, where a few muskets were discharged, by which two soldiers were wounded. The killahdar was made prisoner; many of the garrison were killed; and many, terrified at the approach of the british soldiers with their bayonets, are said to have rushed headlong from the rock.

When in our possession, this place was fitted up as a general hospital, and a magazine for the grain and stores, that could not be carried on immediately with the army. For these purposes it was extremely well adapted, as the lower fort was strong, spacious, and contained a number of good houses. It's situation, too, was convenient, being between forty and fifty miles from Seringapatam.

Home del.t Pittler sculp.t

NORTH VIEW of RAMGAREE.

Published as the Act directs by R. Bowyer, Historic Gallery, Pall Mall, London, & W. Sharp, Madrass, Feb.y 1794

رامکري

رامکري قلع عمده است در میان راه بنکالور و سرنکه پاتام و کویاکه مرکز ان بیشه کلان که از شیوه کنکه تا بدریای کاوري مبسوط است میباشد

کپتان ولش روز بیست و دویم ماه دسمبر سال یک هزار هفت صد نود و یک انکریزي بر قلع پستری و پتهرا حمله اورده هر دو جارا کرفت و در حال قلع دار حواله خود سپرد

RAMGURRY.

Ramgurry is situated twenty-six miles south west from Bangalore, and fifty-one east north east from Seringapatam, on the middle road between those two places. The fortifications occupy a considerable extent, and are very respectable in point of strength; though the place is by no means capable of making such a resistance as Savendroog, or even Outradroog.

The country around has a wild and savage aspect, it abounding with barren rocks, and extensive thickets, the abode of tigers and other beasts of prey. Iron, however, the common product of the sterile soil, that denies man the more genial fruits of nature, is found here in considerable quantities, and applied to that worst of purposes, the fabrication of implements of war. Surely this was not the design of the benevolent creator of the universe! He gave it as an instrument to contribute to the support of life, not to spread destruction around. Where the prolific bosom of the earth spontaneously yields the nutritious and delightful produce of vegetation, the spade and the ploughshare are unnecessary, and iron is not to be found. But where every exertion of art must be employed, to force the barren glebe to fertility, there supreme beneficence has placed the friendly ore at hand, to furnish industry with the implements requisite to render it's toil efficacious.

Like most of the hill forts in the forest between Seringapatam and Bangalore, Ramgurry is much infested with the mischievous tribe of monkeys. They frequently plunder the houses of the inhabitants, devouring their grain and other provision; and their sagacity on these predatory expeditions is astonishing: for, commonly entering through the roof by removing a tile, they first lift it up a little way, and peep in to see the coast clear, before they venture to descend in quest of prey.

Immediately on the taking of Savendroog, captain Welch, who, as we have before observed, commanded the detachment stationed on this road, was ordered to advance and summon the forts of Ramgurry and Shevagurry, by which the road was commanded.

Accordingly, on the 22d of december, 1791, he appeared before this fortress; and, the killahdar refusing to surrender it, he instantly attacked the lower fort and pettah, and carried them by assault. Terrified by the rapidity of the attack, and the facility with which the troops under captain Welch accomplished their purpose, the killahdar at once gave up the place, without farther resistance.

This fortress had but lately been strengthened by new works; and it was found to be well provided with guns, provision, and stores, the chief part of which had been removed from Chenepatam, when that fort was dismantled the preceding year.

Home del.t — Reding sculp.t

EAST VIEW of CHENAPATAM.

Published as the Act directs by R. Bowyer, Historic Gallery, Pall Mall, London; & W. Sharp, at Madras, Feb.y 1792.

حیتپیاتام

این قلع در میان راه بنکالور و سرنکاپاتام است این جارا تیپو لایق حفاظت ندانستند

CHENEPATAM.

THE fort of Chenepatam is situated on the middle or direct road from Bangalore to Seringapatam; from the former of which places it is distant somewhat more than thirty miles, south west half west; from the latter, near forty, east north east.

It not being very conspicuous for it's strength, Tippoo Sultan thought proper to dismantle it, in 1790, and remove it's guns and stores to Ramgurry, which was supposed to be much more capable of defence.

Home delt. Fittler sculpt.

NORTH EAST VIEW OF OLIAHDROOG.

Published as the Act directs by R. Bowyer, Historic Gallery, Pall Mall, London, & W. Sharp, Madrass, Feb. 1794.

Home del. Fittler sculp.

SOUTH EAST VIEW of OLIAHDROOG.

Published as the Act directs by R. Bowyer, Historic Gallery Pall Mall, London & W. Sharp, Madrass. Feb. 1. 1794

Home del. Fittler sculp.

SOUTH EAST VIEW of OLIAHDROOG.

Published as the Act directs by R. Bowyer, Historic Gallery Pall Mall, London & W. Sharp, Madras, Feb. 1, 1794

اولیادروک

قلع اولیادروک کوچک است لیکن بر سنک بلند نهاده روز ۱۹ ماه جون سال ۱۷۹۱ بتصرف انکریزان بیجنک امد حصارهاي قلع شکسته وا کردند تیپو باز مرمت قلع فرمودند و دران سپاه کذاشت روز ۲۷ ماه جانواري سال ۱۷۹۲ باز بدست انکریزان و مهرتهها در امد

OOLEADROOG.

THE fortress of Ooleadroog is small, but situated on an inaccessible rock, so that it may securely bid defiance to any weapons but those of famine.

Notwithstanding it's natural advantages, however, it changed it's master three times in the course of the late war.

On the 19th of june, 1791, the allied armies having crossed the Madoor, and encamped on it's eastern bank, the chief engineer, lieutenant-colonel Ross, was sent forward with the 22d battalion of coast sepoys, commanded by captain Oram, to reconnoitre and summon Ooleadroog; and the day following the 6th brigade was sent to invest the place, and make an appearance of attacking it. Fortunately the garrison thought their enemies too formidable to be resisted, and agreed to yield up the place, on condition of having their private property secured to them, and being safely escorted clear of our camp.

In the neighbourhood of this place were collected above six thousand head of cattle, and two thousand sheep; which, with a quantity of grain in the fort and pettah, afforded a seasonable supply to the army. At the same time were liberated thirty people from the Carnatic, one of whom had been kept in irons in the fort seven years, another fourteen; probably forgotten by the tyrant of the day, as what moti can be assigned for the perpetual imprisonment of a few obscure pea sants brought from a distant country?

Lord Cornwallis, deeming it too inconsiderable to be kept by our army, it was offered to the Mahrattas, as an useful halting place for their convoys: but they also declining it's possession, orders were issued to destroy it, so as to prevent it's being again occupied by the enemy.

After we had thus quitted it, Tippoo thought proper to repair it's dismantled works, and garrison it afresh. This we found, when our army encamped near it, on the 27th of january, 1792, on the march to Seringapatam. A reconnoitering party being sent on from the left wing, the garrison fired upon it, as it approached: but when the kil-lahdar was summoned by lieutenant-colonel Maxwell, who told him, that there was no time to deliberate, for, if he delayed, he should in-stantly commence the attack, he was so intimidated as to surrender without farther resistance.

Ooleadroog was now garrisoned, and established as an advanced post, being ten miles nearer the grand object than Outradroog: and from this place the allied armies, being finally assembled, commenced their march on the 1st of february for the second attempt on Tippoo's capital.

Home del. | Byrne sculp.

VIEW of SHEVAGURRY from the top of RAMGAREE.

Published as the Act directs by R. Bowyer, Historic Gallery Pall Mall London, & Mr Thorp Madras, [illegible]

شیواکری

شیوکری سنگ عظیم محفوظ است اندک دور از رامکری
کپتان ولش زوزیکه رامکری گرفته بود هینجارا نیز
بجنگ و جدل در تصرف خود آورد

SHEVAGURRY.

SHEVAGURRY is a large fortified rock, situated nearly in the centre of that extensive forest, which reaches from Shevagunga to the banks of the Cauvery.

This fort, as well as Ramgurry, from which it is not far distant, was one of those, which, in 1730, were taken from Kempy Gowr, by Deo Rauze.

It surrendered, at the first summons, to captain Welch, on the 22d of december, 1791, immediately after the fall of it's neighbour.

Home del.^t — Byrne sculp.^t

VIEW of SHEVAGUNGA from the road to SERINGAPATAM.

شیواکنکا

در اطراف شیمالي ان بیشه کلان است که تا بکناره دریاي کاوري مبسوط باشد و سرحد حافظ میان بنکالور و سرنکاپاتام میشود

SHEVAGUNGA.

SHEVAGUNGA is situated on the northern border of that ample forest, which, covering a country near seventy miles in length and forty in breadth, extending to the banks of the Cauvery on the south, skirted by the Madoor on the west, and reaching nearly to Bangalore and the ghauts from which the Paneaur descends on the east, opposes a strong barrier to an enemy marching against Seringapatam from the side of Madras.

Through this forest there appear to be but four roads, or defiles, by which an army can pass: and on each of these, as well as throughout the whole extent of this difficult country, are many fortified hills, formerly the castles and possessions of rajahs and poligars, the petty princes and chiefs of the gentoos, but all of them previous to the late war subject to Tippoo, and garrisoned by his troops.

Home delt. Byrne sculpt.

NORTH VIEW of PEDDI-NAIG DROOGUM.

Published as the Act directs by R. Bowyer, Historic Gallery, Pall Mall, London, & W. Sharp, at Madras, Feb. 1, 1794

WEST VIEW of PEDDI - NAIG DROOGUM.

Published as the Act directs, by R. Bowyer, Historic Gallery, Pall Mall, London, & W. Stamp at Madrass, Feb. 1792

پدیناایکدرکم

نام خود میدهد بکذاري در کوههاي مشرقي ميان امبور و ونکاتکيري که بار راه کرنل اولدام در ماه اپرل سال ۱۷۹۱ لشکر بامداد امیر ال امرا لارد کارنوالس کشیدند

PEDDINAIGDURGUM.

Peddinaigdurgum is situated at the head of a pass through the eastern ghauts, between Amboor and Vencatighery, in the midst of a forest, in a wild and rugged country.

Through this pass, after it had been cleared by the exertions of captain Read, colonel Oldham conducted a reinforcement for lord Cornwallis, with supplies of provision and stores. On the 22d of march, 1791, the colonel arrived at Amboor, where he remained till the approach of the grand army; when he advanced through the pass, encamped at Peddinaigdurgum, and the army having arrived, on the 18th of april, at Vencatighery, of which captain Read had previously taken possession, he joined it there, with about 700 europeans, and 4500 native troops, of whom 450 were cavalry, on the following day.

Home del. Stadler sculp.

WEST VIEW of SERINGAPATAM from the middle of the RIVER.

Published as the Act directs by R. Bowyer, Historic Gallery, Pall Mall, London, & W. Sharp, Madrass, Feb. 1794.

Home del. Pollard sculp.

N. N. E. VIEW of SERINGAPATAM from CAPT. SIBBALD'S REDOUBT.

Published as the Act directs by R. Bowyer, Historic Gallery, Pall Mall, London, & Wellsop, Madrass, Feb.y 1, 1794.

EAST VIEW of SERINGAPATAM.

Published as the Act directs by R. Bowyer, Historic Gallery, Pall Mall, London & W. Stamp, Madras, Feb.y 1. 1792.

Home del.t

Fittler sculp.t

NORTH VIEW of SERINGAPATAM.

Published as the Act directs by R. Bowyer Historic Gallery Pall Mall London & W. Sharp Madras Feb.y 1 [illegible]

Home delt. Fittler direxit

DISTANT VIEW of SERINGAPATAM from MEADOWS REDOUBT.

Published as the Act directs by R. Bowyer Historic Gallery Pall Mall London & W. Sharp at Madrass Feby. 1794

Home del.

VIEW of the NORTH EAST ANGLE of SERINGAPATAM.

Published as the Act directs by R. Bowyer, Historic Gallery, Pall Mall, London & W. Sharp, Madras, Feb. 1, [illegible]

سرنکاپاتام

تخت سلطنت تیپو سلطان در جزیره میان دریای کاوری است بر حد مغربي ان جزیره قلع و برجها در اطراف مشرقي باغي کلان و در ان میان دولت خانه وسط مکر باغي خورد بطرف شیمال هکي. معمور بود پیش از جنک کذشته سال ۱۷۹۷ مهرهتهها و نظام دکن با باضی انکریزان محاصره سرنکاپاتام کردند لیکن حیدر علي صلح با مهرهتهها بوسیله مبلغ کران نهودند سال ۱۷۹۲ رفیقان مذکور با لشکر قاهر تابع حکم ارل کارنوالس باز بر شهر مذکور هجوم اوردند و شهر خلاصي نیافتي اکر تیپو سلطان سپردن نصف ممالک خود و ادا کردن سه کرور و سي لک روپیه قبول ننهودي

SERINGAPATAM.

Seringapatam, the capital of the kingdom of Mysore, and of Tippoo Sultan's dominions, derives it's name from the god Serung, or Seryrung, to whom one of it's pagodas is dedicated. It is situated in an island, formed by the river Cauvery, in latitude 12° 25′ 40″ south, and longitude 76° 34′ 30″ east from Greenwich. This island extends about four miles in length, from east to west, and is about a mile and half over, in it's middle or broadest part. The ground in the central part is somewhat more elevated than the rest, and slopes with a gentle declivity towards each end.

The fort and outworks occupy about a mile of the western end of the island; and the laul baug, or great garden, about an equal portion of the eastern. This garden was laid out in regular walks of shady cypress; and abounded with fruit trees, flowers, and vegetables of every kind. But the axe of the enemy soon despoiled it of it's beauties; and those trees, which once administered to the pleasures of their master, were compelled to furnish materials for the reduction of his capital. At the same time the dowlat baug, or rajah's garden, which was situated on the north side of the island, nearer the fort, was undergoing a similar devastation by order of Tippoo, lest that also should be applied to the same purpose.

The whole space between the fort and the laul baug, except the small enclosure, called the dowlat baug, just mentioned, was filled with houses, forming an extensive suburb, of which the pettah of Shaher Ganjam alone remains; the rest having been destroyed by Tippoo to make room for batteries to defend the island, and to form an esplanade to the fort.

This pettah, of modern structure, built in the centre of the island, is about half a mile square. The streets, regularly crossing each other, are all wide, shaded on each side by trees, and full of good houses; and a strong mud wall surrounds it. In all probability this town was preserved for the accommodation of the bazar people and merchants, and for the convenience of the troops stationed in that part of the island for it's defence.

Within the laul baug Tippoo had erected for himself a superb palace, and in the eastern corner of the garden a pleasant bungulo, or summerhouse, looking down the Cauvery, where a junction of those two arms that surround the island is formed. This bungulo and the upper part of the palace afforded excellent accommodations for our sick and wounded officers; as did the lower part of the palace, and the square of faquier's choultries round Hyder's tomb, for the private soldiers.

The fort itself, constructed on the west end of the island, is of a triangular figure. The two branches of the river embrace it on it's longest sides. The base of the triangle, towards the island, being the face most liable to attack, is covered by strong outworks, and defended by two broad and massy ramparts, the second a considerable distance within the first. Each of these ramparts has good flank defences, a deep ditch, with drawbridges, and every advantage of modern fortification. The white walls of the fort, it's regular outworks, magnificent buildings, and ancient hindu pagodas, contrasted with the more lofty and splendid mosques lately raised in honour of the mohammedan faith, of which Tippoo was the zealous apostle, render it a conspicuous object.*

Seringapatam formerly belonged to a pious poligar rajah, who, going on a pilgrimage to Ramisseram, had confidence enough in his neighbour, the prince of Mysore, to leave it in his charge. Having duly atoned, as he imagined, for his sins, he returned to his capital: but the mysorean refused to deliver it up; asserting, that the god Serung had commanded him to retain the government. The new sovereign, backed by the authority of the god, being too hard for the poor pilgrim, he was obliged to relinquish his sceptre, which continued in the family of the usurper for three centuries.

His descendants enlarging their dominions by conquest, Seringapatam ultimately became the metropolis of an extensive kingdom, now known by the general name of Mysore. One of these, marrying into the family of the Cullala poligar, promoted him to the office of delwy, or prime minister; and custom gradually rendered this office, as it has many others, hereditary. In the year 1747, Nundy Rauze, at that time delwy, deposed the rajah Shumca Rauze; sent him prisoner to Kuppaldroog, where he died in confinement; and placed on the throne Kishen Rauze, an infant of the royal family. Under this nominal rajah the reins of government remained entirely in his own hands; and, to render his authority more securely permanent, he gave him his daughter in marriage.

Among other expeditions Nundy Rauze engaged in the dispute between Mohammed Ali and Chunda Sahib; and it was in this service,

* For a plan of the fort and island, and the operations of the siege in february, 1792, see the end of the book.

that Hyder Ali exhibited the first tokens of that courage, skill, and activity, in the command of a body of horse, which were the instruments of his subsequent aggrandizement; enabling him finally to supplant Nundy Rauze, and assume the sovereignty.

Gopaul Row and Bulwant Row, mahratta generals, under Hana, entered Balaghaut in 1756, and gave Hyder an opportunity of displaying his abilities afresh. On this occasion he grew into very high favour with the rajah and Nundy Rauze, who bestowed on him the title of bahauder, and the post of generalissimo. Finally, however, the mahrattas acquired such a superiority, that Nundy Rauze began to despair of an accommodation; when Hyder confidently engaged to procure a peace. Being in consequence invested with full power to treat, and act according to the exigence of the case, he assumed the entire management of public affairs, appointed for his peishkar Kundy Row, originally his slave, mortgaged a great part of the lands for ready money, to buy peace from the mahrattas, gave jagheers to the rajah and Nundy Rauze for their maintenance, and supported the army on the remainder of the revenues.

The mahrattas, having returned to their own country, were not long before they engaged in a war with Sujah Dowlah and other mohammedan powers in the north, and sent the greater part of their forces to Hindustan. An opportunity so favourable was not to be neglected by the politic and active Hyder, who soon reconquered from them all the provinces they had forcibly ravished from the mysorean dominions. This event took place in the year 1760. It completely established his authority, and obtained him fresh honours from his nominal masters.

It was about this period, that Burry Amma, an old woman of the rajah's family, formed the design of depriving Hyder of his power, and restoring the rajah, or rather his minister, to his authority. In this plot she engaged Kundy Row.

Hyder had just returned from an expedition, and encamped on the island, when a cannonade from the fort gave him the first intimation of the plot. Unacquainted with the extent of the danger that menaced him, he fled with a small party to Bangalore, where he collected his troops. Thence returning in full force to Seringapatam, he threatened the place with destruction, unless Burry Amma would deliver up the traitor Kundy Row, that his perfidy might receive it's due punishment. Terrified into compliance, she gave up her wretched tool, who was immediately sent to Bangalore; where, after having been confined a month in an iron cage, the bowstring put an end to his life. Hyder now entered the fort without opposition, and reassumed the reins of government, but made a specious offer of resigning them to Nundy Rauze. He, confiding in his false professions, was weak enough to put himself into Hyder's power; but he soon perceived his errour, when, instead of a palace, he found prepared for him a prison. Thus Hyder attained the summit of authority, and exercised it with despotic sway: though he still affected to rule in the name of the rajah, whom he annually exhibited to the public at the dussarah festival; when, in the true style of oriental hypocrisy, he presented to him a nuzzer, and professed himself his slave.

In 1767 a confederacy was formed against Hyder, to which in all appearance he must inevitably have fallen a victim. After having rapidly recovered all the northern provinces, which Hyder had formerly conceded and afterwards taken from them, a great army of mahrattas, under Mahdoo Row, and another of the soubah's forces, commanded by the nizam in person, and his brother Bazalet Jung, joined by a detachment of british troops, which the government of Madras had agreed to furnish for the expedition, proceeded to attack Seringapatam.

Hyder determined to risk every thing in it's defence, and intrenched himself under the walls, having first laid waste the adjacent country. The plain of Seringapatam was covered with above a hundred thousand cavalry, and more than two hundred elephants, followed by a body of infantry, with about fifty large cannons. They drew off however, on receiving the first discharge of artillery from Hyder's lines; and deeming it impracticable to force a position of such strength, they differed on the measures to be pursued for the farther prosecution of the war. In want both of grain and forage, the mahrattas were bought off by Hyder, and withdrew from the siege. The nizam, too, apprehensive for his safety, agreed to a separate negotiation; which not only terminated hostilities on his part, but ended in his uniting with Hyder, to exterminate the british power in the Carnatic. To this alliance the nizam did not continue true; but it's consequence was a ruinous invasion of our territories, which, though ably opposed by general Joseph Smith, concluded in a disgraceful peace, dictated by Hyder at the gates of Madras, in 1769.

In 1771 the mahrattas again invaded Mysore under Mahdoo Row: but that chief, after various successes, returned to Poonah, and left Trimmuck Row to carry on the war. In this war, Hyder's army was overtaken at Chilcahoorly hill, near the lake of Mooty Tallaow, as he was retreating to his capital, and was totally defeated, with a dreadful slaughter; Hyder himself escaping to Seringapatam, without a single attendant. The total subversion of Hyder's empire must in all probability have followed, but for the friendly interposition of Mara Row, who had considerable influence with the mahratta chiefs. Through his means he was enabled to purchase a peace, at the expence of sixty lacs of rupees; and his own extraordinary abilities enabled him soon to retrieve his affairs.

In 1774 Hyder obtained from Ragobah, who had succeeded to the government of the mahratta country, a grant of all the provinces he had ceded. The chiefs, who governed them, however, refused to give them up: but he expelled them by force, and amongst them even his friend Mara Row. He then turned his arms against the rajahs of Chitledroog and Harponelly, and other poligars, all of whose possessions and treasures he seized.

In 1780 he invaded the Carnatic, with an army of near a hundred thousand men, and threatened utterly to crush the british power on the Coromandel coast; when he was defeated in a pitched battle by sir Eyre Coote, at the head of the remains of our forces, who thus checked his ambitious career.

Hyder Ali Khan died in 1782, and was succeeded by his son Tippoo Sahib, under the appellation of Tippoo Sultan.

In 1790 the mahrattas and the nizam once more united with the british government, to repress the growing power, and curb the restless ambition of the sovereign of Mysore. To enter at large into a detail of every minute circumstance of the war would take up too much room, and we have already recorded some of it's principal events:* we must content ourselves, therefore, with a brief abstract of what more immediately relates to our subject.

* The several occurrences of the war are marked in the general map of the Mysore and Carnatic, at the end of the work.

The british forces were divided into three bodies. One, named from it's position the centre army, commanded by colonel Kelly, was to protect the Carnatic: a second, the bombay army, under general Abercromby, was to reduce the country lying on the west of the ghauts, and then to form a junction with the grand army: the third, under general Medows, was to reduce the Coimbettore country, and then ascend the eastern ghauts. Of the latter army earl Cornwallis in 1791 took the command. The mahrattas and the nizam were to attack the enemy's dominions in the quarters bordering on their's, and proceed on to Seringapatam; where all the forces were to unite, as in one common centre.

It was on the 13th of may, that lord Cornwallis, who had been joined at Cottapilly on the 13th of april by 14 or 15000 of the nizam's troops, pitched his camp at Arakeery, about nine miles east of Seringapatam. Tippoo immediately crossed over from the island, to the north side of the river, and took a position directly in his front, about six miles distant. The ground chosen by Tippoo was such, that he could not be attacked in front but under great disadvantages. To avoid these, lord Cornwallis, who ardently desired to bring him to a general action, marched round some hills on his right, by a circuitous course, on the night of the fourteenth, and came in view of his left wing at eight in the morning of the 15th. This obliged Tippoo to change his ground; though it would still have been sufficiently advantageous, had he not to have contended with troops far superiour to his own; particularly as our army had marched the whole of a wet and stormy night, over bad ground, and the draft cattle were already jaded.

The action was begun by colonel Maxwell, who stormed and carried a height, where an advanced party, commanded by Kummur ul Deen, was posted. On this the main body moved forward, and the action soon became general. Colonel Maxwell, leaving a sufficient force to keep possession of the height, advanced rapidly to gain the ascent of the Carigat ridge, close to the enemy's left flank; and colonel Floyd immediately advanced with the cavalry towards the right. On this the enemy gave way; and our army pursued, till the batteries on the island opened, and checked it's progress. One gun was captured in the field, and three on the height, several colours were taken, and three thousand stands of arms were found on the field after the battle.

Notwithstanding this victory, and though general Abercromby with his army was at hand, provision falling short, and the rainy season, and consequent swelling of the Cauvery, approaching, it was impossible to remain before Seringapatam for the present with any prospect of success. Nay, so exhausted were the draft bullocks, that it was found necessary to destroy the train of battering artillery, previous to retreating towards Bangalore. On the 6th of june, the combined armies, for the mahrattas had joined on the 28th of may, quitted the vicinity of Tippoo's capital.

The intermediate time having been employed in taking such measures as tended to further the grand object of the campaign, on the 5th of february, 1792, the army once more encamped in the neighbourhood of Seringapatam. Tippoo was also encamped under it's walls, on the north side of the Cauvery, within the bound hedge.

On the night of the 6th lord Cornwallis planned a bold attack on Tippoo's fortified camp, which was executed with complete success. It was conducted in three divisions: the right commanded by major-general Medows; the centre under the immediate orders of lord Cornwallis, with lieutenant-colonel Stuart as second in command; the left led on by lieutenant-colonel Maxwell. In this action lord Cornwallis had his left hand grazed by a musket shot.

Though our loss was considerable, it was nothing in proportion to the advantages of the victory; and that of the enemy was of course much greater. It is said, that some days after the battle the sultan's killed, wounded, and missing amounted to twenty thousand; great numbers having deserted in consequence of his defeat. He lost also his camp, and eighty pieces of cannon.

Immediately on gaining this victory colonel Stuart took post on the east end of the island, with a strong detachment, and our grand camp was removed nearer the walls. The island afforded abundance of materials for the siege, and our people began to prepare them with the utmost alacrity. On the night of the 18th the trenches were opened, on the north side of the fort; and in the mean time major Dalrymple beat up the enemy's horse camp, on the south side of the river, in order to draw their attention to that quarter. On the 19th general Abercromby crossed to the south side of the Cauvery.

Tippoo now used every exertion to strengthen his defences; yet, despairing of being able to make any effectual resistance, he seriously turned his thoughts to peace, and lord Cornwallis agreed to receive vakeels with his proposals. The first meeting was on the 15th; a second took place on the 16th; a third, on the 19th; and a fourth, on the 21st. Still the military operations on neither side were suspended; and on the 22d Tippoo made an attack on an advanced party of the bombay army, but was repulsed.

By the 1st of march the two breaching batteries, one of twenty guns, the other of twelve, would have been ready to open; as well as an enfilading battery of at least ten on the south west side of the fort. Adding to these the cross fire that was to be directed from the island and Sibbald's redoubt, with the mortars and howitzers of the train, there would have been a fire of fifty pieces of heavy ordnance against the place; not to reckon any number of smaller guns, that it might have been deemed necessary to employ. Furnaces for heating shot, too, were prepared: so that this extensive fortress, filled with houses constructed of combustible materials, must almost inevitably have been soon in flames.

But in the general orders issued on the 24th of february, the preliminaries of peace were announced, and hostilities were directed to cease.

As hostages for the fulfilment of the treaty Tippoo agreed to give his second and third sons. The elder, Abdul Kalik, was about ten years of age; dark complexioned, with thick lips, a small flattish nose, and a long pensive countenance, yet graceful in his manner, and, when the novelty of his situation wore off, animated in his appearance. The younger, Mooza ud Deen, was about eight; remarkably fair, with regular features, a small round face, large full eyes, and a lively countenance. His mother, a sister of Burham ud Deen, who was killed at Sattimungalum, a beautiful, delicate woman, died absolutely of fear, a few days after the attack of the lines.

On the 26th, about noon, the princes left the fort, mounted on elephants richly caparisoned, seated in silver houders, and attended by their father's vakeels. At the tents sent from the fort for their accommodation, and pitched near the mosque redoubt, they were met by sir John Kennaway, and the vakeels of the nizam and the mahratta chief, also on elephants, who accompanied them to head quarters. The procession was led by several camel hircarrahs, and seven standard bearers, carrying small green flags suspended from rockets, followed by a hundred pikemen, whose weapons were inlaid with silver. Their guard of two hundred sepoys, and a party of horse, brought up the rear. As they approached head quarters, the battalion of bengal sepoys, commanded by captain Welch, appointed for their guard, formed a street to receive them.

Lord Cornwallis, attended by his staff, and some of the principal officers of the army, met the princes at the door of his large tent, as they dismounted from their elephants; and, after embracing them, led them, one in each hand, into the tent. When they were seated on each side of his lordship, Gullam Ali, the principal vakeel, addressed him thus: These children were this morning the sons of the sultan my master; their situation is now changed, and they must look up to your lordship as their father.

Lord Cornwallis, who had received the boys with the tenderness of a parent, anxiously assured the vakeel, and the princes themselves, that every possible attention should be shown them, every possible care taken of their persons.

At this interesting scene the princes appeared in long white muslin gowns, and red turbans. Each had several rows of large pearls round his neck, from which hung an ornament consisting of a ruby and an emerald, of considerable size, surrounded by large brilliants, and in his turban a sprig of valuable pearls. The correctness and propriety of their conduct evinced, that they had been bred up with infinite care, and taught in their youth to imitate the reserve and politeness of age.

The day following lord Cornwallis, attended as before, visited the princes at their tent. Each of them presented his lordship with a fine persian sword; and in return he gave the elder a fusee; the younger, a pair of pistols, of curious workmanship.

Still, however, such difficulties and delays arose on the part of Tippoo, respecting the final adjustment of the definitive treaty, that preparations were made for recommencing the siege, and hostilities were on the point of being renewed. Probably our demand of the Coorga country was the article to which he was most averse; as it prevented him from wreaking his vengeance on the rajah, whom he considered as the chief instrument of the war. To this, however, he found himself obliged to submit; and on the 19th of march the treaty was delivered to the confederate powers, having been signed on the 17th of that month, or the 23d of the month rejeb, in the year of the hejra 1206.

By this treaty half of Tippoo's dominions, affording an annual revenue of one hundred and eighteen lacs and half of rupees, were parcelled out amongst the confederate powers; all the prisoners of the four powers, from the time of Hyder Ali, were to be unequivocally restored; and three crores, and thirty lacs of rupees were to be paid by Tippoo to the allies, half immediately, the remainder by three instalments, of four months each. A perpetual friendship and alliance was also of course agreed upon between the parties.

قبر حیدر علی خان

نزدیک بان باغی کلان در جزیره سرنکاپاتام است در
احاطه مقبر علی و در پیشانی ان صفات برگزیده
بهشت نشین نویسانیده اند در چهار طرف چولتریان
فقرا مبنی و در مقابل مقبر مسجدی خورد بالای
نماز است

THE TOMB

OF

HYDER ALI KHAN.

We cannot better terminate our work than with the proud mausoleum of Hyder Ali: a man whose grandfather is unknown, and whose father, the obscure killahdar of a paltry fort, but for him would have never been remembered.

In the preceding article we have noticed the principal steps by which he rose from his original insignificance to the summit of despotic power: and if talents for governing could confer a title to sovereignty, his claim would be unquestionably strong. Practically, indeed, this title appears in general to have been held good: for, if we examine the various dynasties the pages of history record, we shall find, that, throughout the globe, far the greater part have originated with some man of talents superiour to his fellows, which have enabled him to sway with ability the sceptre he had seized by force. When at length this sceptre has descended by hereditary succession to men, who have supposed that succession a sufficient title, and have neglected therefore to qualify themselves for the office they held, some other, with no claim perhaps but talents of a higher order, struck out from the multitude by the collision of circumstances, or brought near to the throne by accidental causes, has stept into his place; by force ejecting the feeble descendant of kings, or by fraud circumventing the degenerate offspring of a man like himself. Thus did Hyder Ali: and the talents of his son have legitimated his claim of succession to an usurper.

When Hyder died in 1782, his remains were deposited in a tomb at the west end of the extensive garden at Seringapatam; and in honour of this founder of a new race of princes, over it his son and successor erected a superb and magnificent mausoleum. It is surrounded by a square of faquiers choultries, which formed a convenient hospital for the sick and wounded of the british troops, during the siege of Seringapatam, in 1792. Opposite to the front of the mausoleum is a mosque; and in the centre of the front, facing the mosque, is a black marble slab, on which is a persian inscription, in memory of the deceased, couched in terms of extreme hyperbole, whilst the pomp of it's turgid diction is disgraced by a play on words, that to an european must appear highly ridiculous, though a native of Mysore seems to hold it not beneath the dignity of the most serious subjects.

Near the tomb of Hyder Ali another has been more recently erected in memory of Burham ud Deen, the brother of one of Tippoo's wives who fell at Sattimungalum, when that fortress was taken by colonel Floyd, on the 26th of august, 1790.

PLAN OF OOTRADROOG TAKEN BY THE ENGLISH ARMY
UNDER THE COMMAND OF THE R^T. HON^BLE. EARL CORNWALLIS K.G. &c. &c. &c.

December 23rd 1791.